CONNECT WITH YOUR KIDS

*Simple Steps That Can Make
Your Relationships Last*

by
Jim Wideman

Harrison House
Tulsa, Oklahoma

08 07 06 05 04   10 9 8 7 6 5 4 3 2 1

Connect With Your Kids:
Simple Steps That Can Make Your Relationships Last
ISBN 1-57794-640-5
Copyright © 2004 by Jim Wideman
Jim Wideman Ministries
P.O. Box 1214
Broken Arrow, OK 74013

Published by Harrison House, Inc.
P.O. Box 35035
Tulsa, Ok 74153

Contents

Acknowledgments v

Foreword...vi

Introduction ix

Chapter 1   The Making of Leaders 1

Chapter 2   King of the Hill 24

Chapter 3   Follow the Leader 37

Chapter 4   Getting To Know You................................42

Chapter 5   Always the Same 49

Chapter 6   Dare To Be Different 54

Chapter 7   Developing Their Gifts 59

Chapter 8   Entering the Twilight Zone 66

Chapter 9   Saying I'm Sorry 71

Chapter 10   Being Open and Honest 75

Chapter 11   Everybody's Welcome 79

Chapter 12   Respecting Authority 82

Chapter 13   Take a Chill Pill 85

Conclusion..89

Endnotes 90

Acknowledgments

This book is dedicated to the two people who have had more impact on my life than words can explain— my mom, Betty Yancy, and my father-in-law, Arthur M. Spencer. Thanks for all you have put into me and taught me. You two are my heroes. I am so blessed to have parents like you. Also, special thanks to my wonderful wife, Julie. Thanks for making me better at everything! Thanks for believing in me and encouraging me to write this book. And, last but not least, thanks Yancy and Whitney for letting dad talk about you all the time and brag on the wonderful women of God you have become. I am proud of you!

Foreword

I'll never forget the day I began working with children. I've heard others testify that they were "called" to work with kids, but that wasn't the case with me. I was drafted.

I was minding my own business, working with the teenagers at the local church I was attending. One morning as I was about to finish teaching the youth Sunday school class, my pastor came running into the room and said, "Jim, get your Bible and grab your guitar. Go to children's church and don't come out." It turned out to be a long day, an extremely long day. In fact, it was the longest month I have ever spent in an hour and a half.

It's not that I had too many children in comparison to the number of workers helping me. I only had seven kids—six normal kids and a little boy named Bubba. It's not uncommon in Jackson, Mississippi, to have a "Bubba" in children's church. In fact, you can go to the mall in Jackson at anytime and holler, "Hey Bubba," and forty grown men will turn around to see what you want.

Those seven kids wore me out. Afterward, I went to my pastor and said, "How long am I going to have to do this?" His words sent a chill up my spine. "Jim, you're going to have to stick with it until God raises up somebody with a vision."

It just so happened that I was attending a Southern Baptist Bible college in Jackson. Fortunately, in my "Godly Tones 101" class, I had learned how to pray with heavenly intonations. I immediately began in earnest, "Merciful and gracious heavenly Father. Oh God, please give somebody a vision for the children's ministry. Open their eyes, precious Lord. Show them what You want to do in the hearts of children. Let them see the heart Jesus has for children. Give them a vision to work with young boys and girls, and show them how the lives of these dear children can be transformed. Please wake somebody up, Lord!"

After praying that prayer over the next few weeks, I realized that I was the somebody God wanted to raise up with a vision to reach young boys and girls. That was over 25 years ago. Over the years I've tried to quit so many times that it's not even funny. But I can't—I just can't get rid of that vision. Ministering to children is the driving force of my life.

While most people aren't "called" to minister to children, most people marry and have children. All parents have a responsibility to raise their children "...in the training and instruction of the Lord" (Eph. 6:4), and I want to help you to do that.

I trust that as you read and apply the principles in this book, you will restore lost connections with your children. I believe if you begin the training process when your children are young, when they reach the turbulent teenage years and beyond, they will continue to follow after God.

Introduction

In looking over my life, I can point to certain days that are very special to me. Giving my life to the Lord, receiving the Baptism in the Holy Spirit, meeting and later marrying my wife. The day God called me to children's ministry also stands out. There was also a time when three simple words dramatically impacted my life. I will never forget the day as long as I live. I was at my wife's side in the delivery room when the doctor said, "It's a girl."

Let me clarify that. I was standing by my wife's head. I personally believe the region below the knees of a woman who is about to give birth is no man's land, and I was not about to venture in that territory. I never went to medical school. That's why I paid big bucks for a doctor to do the honors. When he announced that we had a girl, I looked at my wife and proclaimed, "All men are jerks." My wife looked at me and said, "What are you?" "I'm a father," I replied.

My view on the American dating system instantly changed. At that moment, I accepted the responsibility to raise a handmaiden of the Most High God. My mission in life became raising a daughter who would know the difference between a man of God and a jerk. I became keenly aware that if I didn't want my child to marry a jerk, *I* couldn't be a jerk. I also realized that I needed to set the example and love her mamma in the same way that I wanted a boy to love her. This became extremely important to me from that day forward; so important that I made major lifestyle changes to accomplish my goal.

Four years later it happened again. I took my wife to the hospital for the birth of our second child. The doctor spoke the same words a second time. "It's a girl." I responded by saying, "I hate men."

I resolved in my heart that I would do whatever it took to develop a relationship with my daughters. If that meant I had to learn how to enjoy shopping or even hand over the television remote to them, then so be it. My daughters are now grown, and I can testify that it *is* possible for a man to do these things. I have come to enjoy watching decorating programs as well as the cooking channel.

On Being a Parent

Life completely changed for me after becoming a father. While the call on my life is to minister to children, I am first and foremost a parent.

I have come to understand that if I reach every child in America but never develop a relationship with my children, I'm missing God. Likewise, if you're too busy establishing your career and never really get to know your own children, or if you're not there for them throughout their lives, your priorities are out of order.

My responsibility as a father and as the priest of my home comes before my ministry responsibilities. God established the home before He established the church. Don't get me wrong. I believe it's important that churches do everything possible to reach the lost, especially children. But it's time that parents rise up and do whatever it takes to reach the kids who are living in their own houses.

The Word backs up this way of thinking. Deuteronomy 6:6-7 says, "These commandments that I give you today are to be upon your hearts. Impress them on your children. Talk about them when you sit at home...." Which children are these verses talking about—the children at church or the children in your home? Unless you take all of the kids in your church home with you, I believe this verse is talking about the children who live with you.

Verse seven continues, "...and when you walk along the road...." (In today's modern translation, that means while driving in the minivan.) "...when you lie down and when you get up. Tie them as symbols on your hands and bind them on your foreheads. Write them on the doorframes of your houses and on your gates" (vv. 7-9). These verses make it very clear that we are commanded to instruct our own children in the Word of God.

We love to quote Ephesians 6:1-3 to our kids. "Children, obey your parents in the Lord for this is right. Honor your father and your mother—which is the first commandment with a promise—that it may go well with you and that you may enjoy long life on the earth." When my mother quoted this verse to me as a child, she usually added, "I brought you into this world, and I can take you out!"

Oh, how we want our children to obey us. However, many parents forget that it is their responsibility to train them and bring them up in the ways of the Lord. While we are commissioned to go to the highways and byways and reach unsaved kids and compel them to come to the Lord, we can't forget about the children who live in our own homes.

Chapter 1

The Making of Leaders

I believe there are two types of people in the world. The first is the person who sees a problem but waits for someone else to solve it. This individual is a follower.

The second type is the kind of person that I want my children to become. I also believe everyone should strive to be this type of person. This personality type is that of a leader.

A leader is a person who comes face-to-face with any type of challenge or problem and solves it. He or she looks to God's Word for direction and approaches the situation by faith. As a result, this person can handle anything.

I've heard my pastor, Willie George, say on many occasions, "Problem solvers go to the head of the line." Do you want your children to be the type of people who always have a job and are considered to be valuable to their companies? If so, train them to be problem solvers.

Parents desire many things for their kids. They want them to have good educations and to be able to get great jobs after college. But I can't think of anything that I would rather my children or the boys and girls that I minister to be than to go to the head of the line and know how to solve difficult problems.

Solving problems was something that Daniel was gifted in. We see in Daniel 5:12 that, "This man Daniel, whom the king called Belteshazzar, was found to have a keen mind and knowledge and understanding, and also the ability to interpret dreams, explain riddles and solve difficult problems."

God is not a respecter of persons, and I don't believe that He loved Daniel more than any other child. If Daniel can be a problem solver, then I believe that any child can have these same abilities.

Choosing Your Problem

I remember when I first started in ministry, I was talking with the pastoral care minister one day. He was a retired senior pastor who had joined our church and did all of the home visitation for us. I began to tell him about a conference I planned on attending. He bluntly interrupted and said, "You don't need to go to that conference. Ask *me* about anything you need to know in ministry."

I thought I would tap into his expertise, so I asked, "Well, what do I need to know?" His answer was simple and profound. "All you need to know is that all churches have problems," he said. "You just need to find the set of problems you want to spend the rest of your life fixing."

I thank God for the problems I've experienced. Even though nobody likes them, they have been a source of growth for me.

Having the Right Attitude

Some people always look at situations the wrong way. They always see the glass as half empty. I like to look at it as half full. I believe we ought to be the kind of people who don't always look at difficulties from a negative viewpoint but look at life with a positive attitude.

Even though you encounter trials and tribulations throughout your life, some of these situations and challenges will cause you to develop character and to grow in your walk with God.

As a result of some of the situations I've encountered, I've learned what to do *and* what not to do. Knowing how to avoid a mistake can be just as valuable as knowing the right choices to make.

I love talking to people who have gone through a building program. I always ask them, "Now that you've completed the construction, if you had to do it again, what would you do differently?" I want to know those things because experience is the best teacher. I don't always have to learn from my own experiences. If I can learn from others, then I don't have to make their mistakes.

I'm from Alabama and am kind of like Forrest Gump. My mamma talked to me about stuff all the time. One of the things she used to say was, "Jim, don't make the same mistake twice. There are plenty of new mistakes you can make for the first time." I've applied this principle to my ministry with children. I've gotten all of the stupid mistakes out of the way. I've learned my lesson the first time around and won't make the same mistake again.

Training Through Adversity

Challenges will make you grow and will help you to be ready for your future. We see an example of this in 1 Samuel 17. This is the story of David's encounter with Goliath. David was someone who learned how to be a problem solver. At an early age he learned how to rely on the wisdom of God and how to make decisions based on God's Word. In looking at his life, you'll see that he didn't start off by immediately handling the tough situations. God first put him in smaller situations that he could handle. These challenges were designed to prepare him for what he would later face. Here is an account of his training.

> David said to Saul, "Let no one lose heart on account of this Philistine; your servant will go and fight him." Saul replied, "You are not able to go out against this Philistine and fight him; you are only a boy, and he has been a fighting man from his youth." But David said to Saul, "Your servant has been keeping his father's sheep. When a lion or a bear came and carried off a sheep from the flock, I went after it, struck it and rescued the sheep from its mouth. When it turned on me, I seized it by its hair, struck it and killed it. Your servant has killed both the lion and the bear; this uncircumcised Philistine will be like one of them, because he has defied the armies of the living God. The Lord who delivered me from the paw of the lion and the paw of the bear will deliver me from the hand of this Philistine."

1 Samuel 17:32-37

The next time you feel like you're facing a lion or a bear, realize that this could be God's way to prepare you for what lies ahead. Most of us, however, are not as good as David. We don't start off fighting lions or bears. Most of us start off with mosquitoes and flies. We then work our way up to rats and cats. Whatever we face, however, God is there to make sure we succeed.

When we've experienced God's faithfulness in small challenges, it helps us to realize that He will be there to help us overcome bigger challenges. It should also help us to see that we don't need to run from adversity. We can face it confidently knowing that we will have the same results as our previous victories.

I heard a Christian song with these lyrics: "If I never had a problem, then I wouldn't know that faith in God would solve them."

Nothing we encounter is too big for the power of God to solve. One of the best things we can teach our children is to face every situation knowing that God is watching out for them. As they step out in the spirit of faith, standing on the promises of God, they can't do anything but be more than a conqueror in every circumstance they encounter. (Rom. 8:37.)

Examples to Follow

As we look in the Bible, we have many examples of problem-solving leaders. Moses, Joshua, David, Joseph, Daniel, and Jesus were all leaders who were great problem solvers.

The common thread among all of these examples is that they were men of prayer who constantly looked to God for direction in every situation they faced. If people today would follow their example of prayer, they would also join the ranks of great problem solvers. It's a parent's responsibility to train their children from an early age to have the good sense to go to God for direction.

Every time I counsel with a young person who has made bad decisions, it can be traced back to the fact that he or she forgot to seek God and search the Scripture to find out what to do in that situation.

Jesus is our best example. Whether He was ministering to the multitudes or to His twelve disciples, He always took time to pray and fellowship with God. His life is a testimony of what prayer can do. He fed the multitude with a few loaves of bread and a few pieces of fish; He raised the dead and laid hands on the sick. These were the good times. Scripture records instances where the Jews sought to kill Him. However, He was able to walk through their midst and escape harm. (John 10:31, 39.)

Training your children to be problem solvers is not difficult. It will take time and consistency. Life will present the challenges. As a parent, your first duty is to show by example how to pray and stand on the Word to overcome the situation. Then, when adversity rears its ugly head in the lives of your children, they can follow your lead. As you give them the necessary support and encouragement, they will learn to never shy away from difficulties but rather to go to the head of the line and be great problem solvers.

Chapter 2

King of the Hill

There are things you can do to ensure that your children are established in the things of God as well as help them to make the right decisions throughout their lives. By continually practicing the steps outlined in this book, you will develop a close relationship with your children that cannot be broken.

If you're reading this book after your relationship with your children has slipped, I believe these steps will help you to reconnect with them.

Number 1: Make Jesus the king of your household.

It is my hope that everyone who reads this book has already made Jesus the Lord of his or her life.*

---

* If you have not accepted Jesus as your Lord and Savior, please go to the back of the book and pray the Prayer of Salvation.

However, have you made Him your king? *A king* is a supreme ruler who controls everything in his kingdom.

Unlike living under the dominion of an earthly king, after you have made Jesus the Lord of your life, it's up to you to decide whether or not you and your household will serve Him. Joshua 24:15 says, "But if serving the LORD seems undesirable to you, then choose for yourselves this day whom you will serve...but as for me and my household, we will serve the LORD." You have to come to the point in your relationship with God that regardless of what anyone else does and no matter what situations in life you face, you and your household will serve God. Only after making this kind of commitment will you have made Jesus king.

Making Him king of your life will also affect every decision you make, what you do and say, how you act and react, and what you allow or don't allow in your home. It will come to a point that you even seek God on whether you should have basic, regular, or premium cable.

I am a firm believer in making Jesus a part of your daily life. While this may sound like a contradicting statement, my wife, Julie, and I don't have family devotions on a regular basis. The reason is simple. I don't think we need to separate our spiritual lives from our everyday lives. Being "a doer of the Word" (James 1:25) is something you should do throughout the day—not just for nightly devotions. Don't get me wrong; I'm not against family devotions. I think it's important that you take advantage of every opportunity to give your children the Word. But if you have to choose between living the Word and conducting nightly devotions, it's better to live the Word.

Pulling Down Strongholds

I define a *stronghold* as simply "believing the wrong information." Unfortunately, there are many strongholds that are formed in the lives of our children. Some strongholds are learned at school, others are learned from friends, while some are passed down from parents. The only way to tear down strongholds is by replacing wrong information with correct information from God's Word. In order to do this, you must teach your kids the Word of God.

Julie and I were strict when the girls were little. I'm sure some people would have said we were overly strict. We guarded the music they listened to as well as the television programs they watched. We never subscribed to HBO or ShowTime through our cable company because we didn't want the girls to even remotely have an opportunity to watch programs on those stations.

As they got older, however, we were able to relax the rules. Why? They never gave us a reason to be strict. As a result, we gave them freedom to make choices. If we saw that they weren't making good choices, we would have had to reestablish the rules. This never happened though because they kept making wise choices.

Leading by Example

My wife and I were born in the 50s, raised in the 60s, and lived through the 70s. When I was young, my hair was about three feet long, and I often shot the peace sign. I had been taught, "Do as I say and not as I do." Kids nowadays don't grow their hair out. Instead, they cut it off. I call them shorthaired hippies. I often tell them to "Get a ponytail," or "Grow some hair."

Unfortunately, kids today don't shoot the peace sign. Instead, they shoot each other. The main thing that has them worked up is the same thing that worked me up as a child, and that is *hypocrites*. Young people don't understand why parents establish rules that they don't follow themselves. You can't hide things from your children. They know what you watch after they go to bed. You have heard the old saying, "If it's good for the goose, it's good for the gander." In other words, you need to practice what you preach. You can't have two sets of rules in your house. Your children will quickly catch on to the double standard. This only opens the door for them to lose respect for you and to rebel against your authority.

Children are looking for someone who will stand up and say, "Follow me as I follow God." Parents should strive to be leaders that are examples to their children. I want to instill my beliefs in my children to the point that they are exhibited in the music they listen to, the television programs they watch, the conversations they have, and the movies they see.

Friends

Parents are quick to say to their kids, "Choose your friends wisely," but whom do you hang out with? Do your friends edify you and build you up in the things of God? You need to choose your friends just as wisely as you want your children to. You are the leader and head of your household and have to set the example for them to follow.

Don't allow your friends to rob you from your family. I have witnessed parents who have spent more time with their friends than with their children when their children were young. The parents were so busy developing relationships with their friends that they never took the time to develop relationships with their children. The children later followed in their parents' footsteps. When they reached their teenage years, they were too busy hanging out with their friends and were not interested in being with their parents. Their behavior, however, was patterned after their parents.

Spending Time With Dear Old Dad

When the girls were little, I spent every available hour I was not working with them. My family was a priority to me, and spending time with my children came before spending time with friends. Today, I am reaping the rewards of my investment.

My daughters are now grown, and they still invite dear old dad to go to the movies with them. My daughters' friends even think I'm cool and want to hang out with me. Some of my daughters' friends have commented that they have a better relationship with me than they do with their own fathers. That's because their dads have not invested time in them. The time I spent with my daughters while they were young was an investment of love that is now paying rich dividends.

The Ultimate Gift-Giver

I'll be honest with you. When my kids were small, I was not thinking about what the payoff would be down the road. I just knew that my wife and I had to be examples of the Word to them. It's really simple. If you want your kids to be doers of the Word, then *you* must be doers of the Word. The way you treat your children will be the same way they look at God.

If you don't want them to think that God is cheap, don't be cheap yourself. I have always tried to be a giving dad because Father God is a giving dad. John 3:16 says that God loved the world so much that He gave. Giving is a natural response from a loving father to his children.

Matthew 7:11 says, "If you, then, though you are evil, know how to give good gifts to your children, how much more will your Father in heaven give good gifts to those who ask him!" Some of the children I know can't relate to that Scripture because their parents never gave good gifts to them. The reason why my kids know that God will take care of their needs and give them the things they need and desire is because, as a father, I have demonstrated to them that their needs and well-being will always be taken care of.

I encourage you to give your kids whatever they need. I didn't say give them *everything they want,* but that's not bad either. Many of us want God to give us the things we want as well as the things we need. I want to be that kind of father to my girls. I want to lavish my daughters with gifts.

The Example To Follow

My biological father was killed in a car accident when I was three, so I never had a dad while growing up. Throughout my childhood I prayed for a father; and when I was seventeen, my mom married my step-dad. He was a wonderful, godly man, and I loved him with all my heart. He's in heaven right now, too.

As a child, I didn't know what it was like to have a father. I didn't know what dads were supposed to do. When I began to read the Bible after I got saved, I saw how God acted as a father, and I came to the conclusion that that's how dads are supposed to be. The best thing parents could strive to do is to imitate Father God.

I looked to God as my example, and I see throughout the Bible that He loved us so much that He *gave*. I also read in Hebrews 11:6 (KJV) that He "…is a rewarder of them that diligently seek him," so I decided that I should give to my kids and reward them when they do good things. I encourage you to look for reasons to bless your kids on a regular basis.

I believe that God is always looking for someone He can bless. If our heavenly Father is that way, why shouldn't a godly earthly mom and dad be the same way? God demonstrated and communicated His love to mankind while we were yet sinners. (Rom. 5:8.) In other words, we don't deserve the love God shows us. He didn't wait until our rooms were clean, or when we made good grades to show His love to us.

Likewise, why don't you follow your heavenly Father's example and show love to your children, even when they don't deserve it?

Love Is...

You may be wondering how you're supposed to show love to your children. My pastor, Willie George, often says that kids don't spell love, L-O-V-E. They spell it T-I-M-E and M-O-N-E-Y. It's important that they receive both from you.

Children need to spend time with their parents, and there are plenty of things you can do that will cost you time. Hiking through the park, perfecting their fastball or jump shot, doing science experiments, pitching a tent and sleeping in it with them, are just a few ways to spend time with your kids. The money part is easy. Children can easily come up with ways for you to spend money. The important thing is to be involved in your children's lives from the beginning.

You need to realize that you have to demonstrate and communicate your love to your family every day, and not just when it's convenient or when you feel like it. I purposed in my heart that my wife would never live a day without hearing me say, "I love you." When God gave me my precious girls, I was determined to have a close relationship with them because I remembered hearing a statistic that stated that 95 percent of all teenage girls who are promiscuous do not have good relationships with their fathers.

If you don't want your children to be featured on a *Girls Gone Wild or Spring Break: Live From Cancun* video, you better build a close relationship with them. If you would interview any of these girls, you would discover that their relationships with their fathers are not healthy or that they are nonexistent. It's because they don't have a proper relationship with a loving father that they are seeking attention from any man who will give it.

One day when my oldest daughter, Yancy, was meeting with a record executive, I called her on her cell phone. She took my call and explained that she was still in the meeting and would call me back. Before she hung up, she told me, as she has always done all of her life, that she loved me. I responded with my typical, "I love you, too," and we hung up. When the record executive heard a girl in her twenties vocally express her love to her father, he was blown away. Yancy didn't know this type of behavior wasn't normal. For the next half hour, they talked about parenting instead of music.

Becoming a vital part of your children's lives is a part of making Jesus the king of your household. When you live as godly examples before your children, then Proverbs 22:6 will come to pass in your household. "Train a child in the way he should go, and when he is old he will not turn from it."

Chapter 3

Follow the Leader

In my observation of married couples, I often hear the husband or wife say that their spouse is just like their mom or dad. I'm sure that young people don't set out to marry someone like their mom or dad, but the qualities that children see exhibited in their parents are what they are usually drawn to.

Number 2: Love your spouse the way you want your children's spouse to love them.

My wife went to Mississippi to visit her dad after he had a stroke. While she was there, she spent some time with her childhood friends. After she got home, she said, "Thank you for adoring me." When she compared her marriage to that of her friends, she was convinced that she had the better deal. She didn't have the biggest house or the nicest car, but she knew that I loved and adored her more now than when we were first married.

Every married couple needs to live by this rule: Whatever you did to win your spouse's affection is the same thing you must do to keep it.

If you bought your wife flowers before you married her, keep sending her flowers afterward. If you asked her out on dates beforehand, don't stop going on dates now that you're married, and especially after you have children. You shouldn't assume that just because you've been married for twenty years that your wife will still want to go out with you. Open the door for her. Buy her nice things. Spoil her every chance you get!

Ladies, you must do the same thing. If you didn't nag your husband before you got married, don't nag him afterward. You overlooked his faults the entire time you were dating, so why are those things bothering you now? If you liked to surprise him by cooking his favorite meal, keep doing that.

Showing Love and Affection

Julie and I have always been very affectionate. The girls have grown up watching us kiss each other every time we get a chance. We kiss each other when saying goodbye as well as when saying hello. We kiss each other before going to bed at night and waking up in the morning. Anytime it's appropriate, we sneak in a kiss. Whitney and Yancy know that I think their mamma is the cat's meow! They have caught us holding each other in the kitchen. They've watched us slow dance to songs on the radio. I'm still head over heels in love with my bride after all these years, and my daughters know it. All of our smooching and affection was normal to them.

When the girls began to date, if the young man they liked didn't show them the same attention that I showed their mother, they thought something was wrong with him and eventually would give him the boot. One of the nicest complements I've ever received was paid to me by one of the young men in our church.

A young man had a crush on my youngest daughter and was asking advice from some of his band mates about how often he should call Whitney. One of the guys told him, "Dude, she's a Wideman girl. She's used to lots of attention." When I heard that, I knew I had accomplished what I had set out to do. I have always tried to set the example of how I wanted others to treat my daughters. I tried to set the bar high for the men who would marry them. I now have my first son-in-law. He's a good-looking young man, hard working, as well as a real gentleman. What I like the most about him is that he has convinced me that he is as crazy about my daughter and adores her in the same way that I adore her mother.

Good or bad, the way you treat your spouse is what your children will grow up to believe is normal. If you show your spouse respect, your children will demand respect from their spouses. On the other hand, if parents rarely speak or yell and scream to get their point across, their children will learn to communicate by either clamming up or by yelling. Children who grow up in homes where little affection is shown often have a hard time showing affection as adults. This is why children who are raised in abusive homes will often marry someone who is abusive. It's the only way of life they know.

Chapter 4

Getting To Know You

All too often, people get caught up in building their careers, pursuing hobbies, starting a business, or even volunteering at church. The list can be endless. God, however, is into families, and spending time with your spouse and children should come before all of the above activities.

Number 3: Spend time with your kids.

Ephesians 5:15-17 says, "Be very careful, then, how you live—not as unwise but as wise, making the most of every opportunity, because the days are evil. Therefore do not be foolish, but understand what the Lord's will is." What is God's will here? To keep your priorities in order.

Getting To Know You

What do you think the first priority in your life should be? If you said *Jesus,* you're correct. After accepting Jesus as your Lord and Savior, reading and studying the Word and growing in the Lord should be your first and foremost priority. Having a personal relationship with the Lord will change your life. It will make you a better person all around and will also help to improve relationships with family members, friends, and coworkers.

Your spouse should be your second priority. I like what my friend Joe McGee, said, "Kids are just passing through, but marriage is forever." Children can be demanding and try to move up on the priority list, but it's important to remember that your spouse comes before your kids. That places your children as your third priority.

In God's design for the family, you first have to develop your relationship with Jesus. Then you must work on your relationship with your spouse. And finally, a relationship with your children needs to be cultivated.

Time Well Spent

When the kids were young, I purposed in my heart that I was going to make time for them every day. Now that they are grown, I try to regularly talk to them on the phone if I can't see them in person. I even have dates with my daughters. One of my rituals is to have Saturday lunches with them. I try to include both of them; but sometimes because of their schedules, one of them will have to miss. It really blesses me when I hear them say, "I've really missed my Saturday lunch with you, Dad."

It started after Yancy was weaned, and I began to take her to puppet practice with me. Julie home-schooled the girls. Since she was with them all week, Saturday became her day to have "alone" time and my day to have some great "dad" time. I continued the Saturday ritual with them on a regular basis. Now that they're grown, they still include me in their Saturdays, and I appreciate that.

Make a point to spend time with your family on your day off, and make it fun for your kids. As a children's pastor, I work hard to make children's church a fun place for the kids. If I do this for children's church, why can't my house be fun as well?

I did some pretty bazaar things when the girls were young. I used to talk to them in imaginary languages. I acted as though I was talking to them in sign language, even though I don't know how to sign. I constantly tried to freak them out. Now that they're older, I haven't changed my ways. I enjoy playing tricks on them by trying to disguise my voice on the phone. We had fun together while they were growing up, and we still do all kinds of things together.

Doing Things Together

Here's a true confession. I didn't really enjoy *The Care Bears Movie,* but I got excited when I read the credits and found out that John Sebastian of the *Loving Spoonful* and Carole King wrote the music. It blew me away that a couple of old rockers would be interested in writing music for an animated movie. How do I know this? Between my wife and me, we have seen all of the movies our children have seen. We let them pick out the movie or concert they wanted to attend, and then either both or one of us went with them. As a result, my wife has attended a Hanson concert as well as more than her fair share of boy bands. On the other hand, I've gone to more ballet recitals than I really want to talk about. For the dads who don't think they can stomach this, remember that Jesus will help you with things like this and much more.

When my oldest daughter got married, I helped plan the wedding. I didn't know when I joined in on the planning that it would be considered weird. I've gone shopping for all kinds of dresses while my daughters were growing up. Shopping happens to be one of the things my family likes to do together. We organized a two-day shopping extravaganza in Dallas to look for a wedding dress. When I went into the bridal shops with my wife and daughter, the salespeople freaked out. "We're not used to having dads," they said. I didn't understand why someone would have such a hard time with a dad helping to pick out something as special as a wedding dress.

We celebrate Christmas and Easter every year, and I've bought plenty of holiday dresses. A wedding is a one-time event, and I wanted to be there. I paid the tab for the extravaganza, and I wanted to know up-front how much it would cost.

After successfully making it through my first wedding, I have some smart advice for dads.

Early in the planning stages of the wedding, my daughter gave my wife and me a long list of everything she wanted for the special event. As she revealed her plans to have the wedding of her dreams, I could only think about the money it was going to cost me. The more she talked, I could only hear cha-ching, cha-ching, cha-ching. Finally, the Holy Ghost gave me a great idea.

I told my daughter, "Listen, here's a set amount of money. It's yours. You can have this money for the wedding or spend it anyway you want. If you don't want to spend all of it on the wedding but would rather keep some of it for appliances or to put toward a house, you can do that. Use this money anyway you want."

When it became her money and not daddy's money, things that were once very important suddenly became not so important. Among other things, the live band went out the window and became CDs. This is the best parenting tip I could give you. You fathers of daughters will thank me for it.

The bottom line is to become involved in your children's lives from the beginning. Many parents get caught up in providing for their children and neglect spending time with them. When placed on a balance, time with your children far outweighs working long hours to make money to buy things for them.

Chapter 5

Always the Same

Many parents wonder why their children listen better to others than they do themselves. They don't realize that they are the prime culprits in what their kids get away with. Children quickly learn how far they can push their parents. That is why many kids don't move until they hear their parents yell. Their parents never "made" them do anything until they screamed. They could have taught their kids to immediately obey by enforcing their discipline immediately.

Number 4: Be consistent in your discipline.

I don't believe there is such a thing as a problem child. I meet children with problems. But just because a child has a problem doesn't mean he or she is bad. In many cases, I've found that they are just confused. In digging deeper into their personal situations, I've discovered that they did not fully understand what the rules were.

I know good parents who are strict and others who are equally as good but who are lenient in their discipline. Neither discipline style is better than the other. What makes good parents is consistency in discipline. Whether strict or lenient, their homes have a consistent structure and their children clearly understand what they are permitted and not permitted to do.

Years ago, when I first began in children's church, I got into the habit of letting the kids know what the classroom rules were. I let them know what I expected them to do and told them what my response would be if they didn't obey the rules. Many children tested the system; but when they saw that I kept my word and that I was consistent in my discipline, they respected the rules and did what they were asked. It amazed the parents that their children acted better in church than at home. Consistency is an important lesson for parents to learn.

Discipline Pointers

In addition to consistency, here are a few pointers that parents sometimes overlook when disciplining their children.

You must always explain to your children why their actions were not acceptable. You need to show them what the Word of God says about their choices and their actions. After your have disciplined them, don't forget to pray with them; and most of all, hug them and let them know that you love them.

You should never discipline out of anger. Even though your child may have done something that sent you over the edge, walk away until you can get a hold of your emotions. If you don't, you will probably say or do something that you will later regret. If this happens, it will be necessary for you to go back to your child and apologize, not for the discipline, but for the "way" in which it was delivered. Disciplining out of anger only draws a wedge between you and your child's relationship.

A United Front

God said in Genesis 2:24 that a man would leave his father and mother and would cling to his wife. Marriage would cause the two to become one flesh. A husband and wife are no longer two separate entities; they are one. God's plan is that they would be united. Becoming one also means that the two are in agreement concerning the affairs of their household.

Where children are concerned, presenting a united front is important. Parents cannot afford to be divided on the disciplining of their children. There were times when my wife and I went into another room so we could get on the same page. It's important that your kids see the two of you saying the same thing. Remember, children rule in a divided home.

It's also important that you support your spouse when he or she makes a discipline decision when you are not there. You only undermine your parental authority if you reverse your spouse's discipline—not to mention disrespecting him or her.

Always the Same

Kids know what they can get from each parent, and they can be adept at getting what they want by playing one parent against the other. There have been times when I've told my kids, "I need to speak with your mom before I give you an answer." Doing this ensures that you and your wife are always united and consistent in the discipline of your children.

Chapter 6

Dare To Be Different

Imagine a world of one color. Blue, red, or green. If that were the case, the sky would blend into the earth. Instead of a world of variety, everything would be bland.

When you look at the intricacy in which God made the earth and everything in it, you'll see that He liked variety. He never made one kind of anything. There are many different types of trees, fish, and animals. You name it, there's more than one type of everything. The same is true with people. They come in all shapes, colors, and personalities. In studying God's mode of operation, you'll realize that He intended it to be that way.

Number 5: Recognize that God created your children differently, and allow them to be different.

If I hadn't been in the delivery room during the birth of my daughters, I wouldn't have believed that they were sisters. They don't look anything alike, and their personalities are completely different. God gave them different giftings and abilities.

Even as a very young child, Yancy never liked toys. When other children begged their parents to take them to Toys "R" Us, she begged us to take her to Office Depot. She's always "worked." Right now, she's involved in four businesses. She runs one and owns three. In addition to all of that, she also works in the music ministry at our church. She's the president & CEO of two corporations. She has an LLC (Limited Liability Company) and a 501(c)(3) (a non-profit tax exemption).

She's always been focused on her goals and loves everything she does. She wrote the song, "I Don't Want to Go," for the gospel group Avalon. It was on their *Oxygen* album; and when it was first released, it ranked number one for five weeks in a row. It became one of the 25 most performed Christian songs in 2002. She's always been an entrepreneurial kind of girl.

On the other hand, my youngest daughter, Whitney, is the complete opposite. She never wanted to work; she's always wanted to play. Her favorite toys were her dolls, and her favorite doll was Barbie. Whitney could play with her Barbie dolls for hours.

Now that she's older, she wants to look like Barbie. She loves fashion, hair, and makeup. Whitney's goal in life has always been to be a wonderful wife and mother. It's only been in the last few months that she has even talked about having some sort of career. She's currently working toward getting an esthetician license to be a make-up artist. Before she made up her mind to go to college, she worked at our church as a receptionist and manager of the youth bookstore.

Not too long ago, I overheard them discussing their future. Yancy said to Whitney, "I wouldn't want to go to work and have a job where I clocked in every day. I want to work for myself." Whitney looked at her and said, "I just want to wake up in the morning and have a place to go—like everybody else in America." They're different, and there's nothing wrong with that.

Encouraging Individuality

A common mistake parents make is that they compare their children to each other. This can cause one child to feel inferior to the other; and as a result, he may spend most of his life trying to live up to the achievements of his sibling and never discover God's plan for his life. You should never try to make your kids to be alike. Let them be who they are.

Equally as bad is when you compare your children to yourself. Parents often clash with the children who are just like they are. That's because they can clearly see in their child the things they don't like about themselves. The things that seem to frustrate me the most about my children are the parts of their personalities that are like mine. They can't help it; it's genetic. You can only try to help them to get over being you. That's what I've been trying to do all my life with my daughters.

Life is so much easier when I accept the things I can't change and change the stuff I can. I am glad that my children are different. They were a blast to raise and to be around. They are truly the bright spots in my life, and I would have missed out on a lot if I had tried to change either one of them.

Chapter 7

Developing Their Gifts

God is a great encourager. He lets us know that we are more than conquerors through Him (Rom. 8:37) and that He will always be with us in whatever we set our hands to do. (Heb. 13:5.) Anytime you need to hear from Him, you can go to His Word and find the answer you need. As parents, it's important that you do the same with your children.

Number 6: Encourage your children to develop their natural giftings.

Proverbs 22:6 says, "Train a child in the way he should go…." One of the definitions for the word *way* is "characteristic, regular, or habitual manner or mode of being, behaving, or happening."[1] A person's *manner* is their "characteristic or customary mode of acting,"[2] or what they are naturally gifted to do. It's up to parents to recognize these natural talents and train and encourage their children to develop these gifts.

Discover and Develop Their Gifts

All too often, parents want their children to fulfill their own unfulfilled dreams, or they want their kids to follow their footsteps. You may love being a bean counter, but that doesn't mean your children have to be accountants.

I don't want my children to stand before God and say, "I wanted to play the guitar and be a worship leader, but my cheap father wouldn't pay for guitar lessons." I once had a child in children's church who loved guitars. I grew up loving guitars, and I love kids who love guitars. I have several guitars and would use a different one each Sunday. This kid would come up to me after class and say, "That's a Les Paul," or "That's a Stratocaster."

He wanted to play guitar so bad he could taste it. God spoke to my heart and said, *Buy him a guitar.* I called his parents and told them my desires, as I wanted their permission before doing so. They gave me their okay and seemed excited about God's provision for their son's dream. I encouraged them to get him lessons and even recommended some instructors. They thanked me and told me they would follow my advice.

The young man loved the guitar I bought him. That's all he talked about. His parents wrote me a letter thanking me for the guitar and even wrote a nice letter to my pastor. Unfortunately, they never kept their word about the guitar lessons. Every time I saw him, he asked questions about how to play the instrument. When I asked if he was taking lessons yet, his countenance would change from excitement to defeat. His parents wouldn't give him lessons. They were not willing to encourage him in his natural giftings.

He's in the youth group now but doesn't attend church. His parents come to church regularly, but he doesn't really care about the things of God. I know why. His parents wanted him to become excited about the things they were interested in and wouldn't encourage him in the things that he liked.

Using Your Talent for God

I've only had two types of jobs. I've worked in bars, and I've worked in churches. My heroes have always been hippies. I have always been fascinated with anyone who could make a living at playing the guitar. The reason I began to play in bars was because the church I attended while growing up didn't encourage me to use my talents for the Lord. They had a pipe organ in the church and felt that if you couldn't play the organ, they couldn't use you. Every now and then, they would let me play my guitar. Bars, however, opened their arms wide and let me come in.

Once I began to work in the ministry, I purposed in my heart that no kid in my children's church would ever have to go to the bars to use their musical gifts and talents. That's why I have several worship bands. Whenever I find out that a child can play a musical instrument and wants to develop his or her talent, I make sure an opening in one of the bands becomes available.

Making an Impact

A former student of mine who's now playing football at Tulsa University introduced me to his girlfriend. I used to pick him up and take him to church for several years because he wanted to play drums in one of the bands. His parents wouldn't bring him to the early service because they liked to attend the eleven o'clock service. They said, "If he's going to play at the nine o'clock service, you'll have to pick him up." So I did.

When a former student introduces his girlfriend to his old children's church pastor, you know it must be serious. He paid me a wonderful compliment that day. He told his girlfriend, "I have a dad, but Brother Jim is the person I go to when I need advice." Even though he's in college, I still have input in his life because I was willing to encourage him in his natural gifting when he was a child.

If this works with kids who are not yours, why not encourage your own children in the things of God.

My youngest daughter, Whitney, has been playing the drums for a couple of years. When she first started, I bought her a practice set so she could keep the drums in her room. After she graduated from high school, she wanted a real set. The set I bought her is what I would have wanted if I were a drummer. I treated her the way I would have wanted to be treated.

Spurring Your Kids On to Greatness

It's important to encourage your children to develop their natural talents. The word *encourage* means "to inspire with courage, spirit, or hope; to spur on; to give help or patronage to."[3] Parents need to support their children in the things that they like. That can mean anything from getting them music lessons, private coaching, cooking classes, or buying them a camera. It's doing whatever it takes to help develop them in their natural giftings.

I've gone with Yancy to see accountants and lawyers. I can also tell you about every cosmetology school in Tulsa because I helped Whitney research them. Students and staff alike looked at me oddly when I toured the beauty school with my daughter, but it meant the world to Whitney.

I may know more about eye makeup than I would like to admit, but that's all a part of being a father and becoming involved in my children's lives. One of the benefits of encouraging them to finding the path that God planned for them and getting involved in the things they like to do, is that they still come to me for advice even though they are grown and have lives of their own.

Chapter 8

Entering the
Twilight Zone

I'm not sure when the phrase "terrible twos" was coined, but personally, I didn't mind those years. Even though you had to constantly watch your children in order to save your home from destruction, the toddler years were easy. Your main advantage over kids that age is that you're bigger than they are. You can always pick them up and put them where you want them.

Something happens to kids when they get older, especially during the preteen and the teenage years. They suddenly become "all knowing" and are convinced that you know nothing. This is the time when all parents will have to deal with the "generational gap." In order to stay connected during these years, you're going to have to venture into their world.

Number 7: Learn about your child's world.

Every time I travel to a foreign country, I try to learn as much as I can about the culture before I go. Several years ago I had the opportunity to minister in Greece. When I met with my missionary contact, he told me that in the Greek culture, forcefully showing the palm of your hand was considered offensive. It has the same meaning as flipping the middle finger in America. This Pentecostal boy needed to know that information. The last thing I wanted to do was to offend the congregation if I raised my hand in praise to God while I was preaching.

After I came back from that trip, I realized that I should show my children the same respect and learn about their culture. I always encourage parents to step into their children's world and dare to find out what interests them.

Youth Culture 101

You can't learn about today's culture sitting in the family room watching reruns of the shows you watched as a child. If you want to learn about your children's world, tune in to any sitcom on TV today or watch MTV. You'll get a good understanding of the likes and dislikes of today's culture.

It's good to at least have knowledge of the music your kids listen to and to know what's in style. If you don't, you'll soon feel as though you're of another generation and a continental divide will separate you from your children.

Finding Out What's Important

How do you get your kids to open up to you? That's easy. The first step is to ask. Talk with them. Go shopping with them. Spend time with them and allow them to tell you their true feelings.

The second step is to not freak out when they answer you. Don't overreact when they express views that are different from yours or that you feel are totally wrong. If you freak out while they're talking, they won't listen to anything else you say. Wait until the discussion is over, go into another room, and freak out on your wife. You can't be a "freaker" if you want your kids to talk to you.

In order to stay "current" on today's generation, I also read entertainment magazines and watch shows like *Entertainment Tonight* and the *People's Choice* award shows.

My kids like many different styles of music, which even includes music that I like. I think one of the reasons they have accepted my music is because I have tried to learn about their music and have accepted what they like.

Taking the Lead

Malachi 4:6 states, "He will turn the hearts of the fathers to their children, and the hearts of the children to their fathers...." This Scripture shows us that the fathers must turn their hearts to their kids first. Many parents aren't willing to do this. They want their children to make the first move. This verse is very plain. When fathers turn their hearts toward their children, the children will return to their fathers.

The pre-teen years are some of the most important developmental years of your children. This is the time they decide what type of person they will be. This is also a time when you want to stay connected to them and have input in their decisions. Learning about their world doesn't have to be like entering the twilight zone. It can be fun and exciting as you take a genuine interest in their lives.

Chapter 9

Saying I'm Sorry

As a parent, saying you're sorry can be tough because you have to first lay aside your pride and admit that you were wrong. We all know people who have refused to say those two simple words. They haven't spoken to family members or friends for years. Sometimes the feud has gone on for such a long time that they don't even remember what caused the rift in the first place. You have to ask yourself, is being "right" worth the loss of a friendship?

Number 8: Admit your mistakes; and when you're wrong, make corrections.

No one is perfect, so admit it when you're wrong. Your kids know it when you make mistakes concerning them. If you refuse to listen to them when they try to explain what "really" happened, you'll only drive a wedge in your relationship. Once they realize that you're not open to hearing what they have to say, they'll stop trying to explain; and eventually, they will quit talking altogether.

Remember, you're the role model. If you will never admit that you've made a mistake, don't expect your children to. However, if you allow the Word of God to bring correction to your life and quickly make changes, your children will follow your example.

Changing Your Ways

I have made a lot of mistakes as a parent. I've jumped to conclusions before getting all the facts; I've lost my temper; and I've said things that I shouldn't have. Time and again, I've had to ask my children to forgive me. The great thing is that they always do. They don't respect me because I'm perfect; they respect me because I'm willing to repent.

There is a difference between saying I'm sorry and repenting. Many children don't know the difference because their parents aren't willing to show them. *Repent* means "to turn from sin and dedicate oneself to the amendment of one's life; to feel regret or contrition; to change one's mind."[4] You can tell your children that you're sorry but never make any attempts to change your ways. That means you still don't listen to them when they're talking; and you continue to make excuses for not showing up at their dance recitals, band concerts, or football games. The list could go on. One thing is for sure, you need to keep your word when you apologize.

An Example To Follow

Actions speak much louder than words. I can tell my children they need to make corrections in their lives, but I also need to model that behavior in my own life. If I tell my kids to pick up after themselves, that needs to be my habit as well. If you don't want your kids to drink, smoke, or swear, then make sure you don't do any of those things.

An area of my life I have struggled with for years is my weight. As I am getting older, I've come to realize that it's not about being thin; it's about being healthy. I can't tell my daughters to eat healthy and exercise if I continually do the opposite. I have made an about face in that area; and because I set the pace for making corrections in my life, I have seen my children making healthy lifestyle choices as well.

The benefits of admitting you're wrong far outweigh the need to be right. Simply saying you're sorry will mend a lot of hurts. It will keep the door of communication open and enable you to work through disagreements to a peaceable end.

Chapter 10

Being Open
and Honest

I encourage you to develop an open-door policy in your children's lives early on. They should feel as though they can tell you anything. Likewise, you should be open about your life and the mistakes you have made over the years.

Number 9: Talk to your children about everything.

I know parents who have never told their children about the mistakes they made while growing up. I, on the other hand, have told my girls everything. They know all of the temptations the devil brought my way and the stupid things I did. They know I did drugs and that I can't remember my junior year in high school because I was high every day that year.

The reason I wanted my girls to know about my past is because I'm smart enough to know that the devil will tempt them with the same things that I was tempted with. If I act as though my past never happened, I'm not preparing them for the temptations they will face. Listen, the devil's not smart. In fact, he's quite stupid. He can't come up with anything new, so he uses the same temptations generation after generation.

Breaking Generational Curses

My real dad died when I was three, and I don't remember him at all. However, I was just like him. We fought the same demons. He never did drugs, but he did alcohol.

He had trouble being faithful to my mom, and I've always liked the ladies—just like dear old dad. In high school, I thought I had to have a date every Friday, Saturday, and Sunday. My philosophy was the more the merrier. After I got saved, I realized I had to break that generational curse in my family if I didn't want my kids to be the same way. I come from a long line of party folks, but I decided to nip that spirit in the bud. My family and I were going to honor God.

Hold Your Horses

Whenever I counsel couples before they get married, I always tell them, "You better not have sex before you say, 'I do,' because you're going to have kids who will grow up to be teenagers. One day they will ask you, 'Did you wait until you got married to have sex?' If you don't want to tell them that you couldn't wait, then get a hold of your hormones and keep your clothes on!" I'm so glad my wife and I waited until we got married to have sex. It's much easier to tell your kids to follow your example rather than to have to explain why your actions were wrong.

Everything Will Be Okay

I'll be honest with you. Even though I had an open-door policy with the girls, I used to flip out a lot when they first started telling me stuff, and I had to learn how to stay calm when I wanted to scream.

One of the most important things that you can instill in your heart as well as in your children's hearts is: The Greater One lives on the inside of your children (1 John 4:4), and He will lead them by His Word and by His Spirit to the right solution. (John 16:13.)

When you recognize that the Greater One lives on the inside of your children and that there isn't any problem that's too big for God, you will have peace and assurance that God has a solution to *whatever* they tell you. And once you turn the problem over to Him, everything will work out just fine. Once I realized this, I didn't flip out anymore and eventually became a really "cool" dad.

Chapter 11

Everybody's Welcome

In most neighborhoods, there is always one house where all of the neighborhood kids hang out. That's the way my home was when the girls were growing up. While many parents are glad for the peace and quiet and are not at all interested in having their house torn up by a bunch of rambunctious kids, I wanted to know what my kids were doing and whom they were doing it with.

Number 10: Make your children's friends welcome in your home.

You want your home to be the house where your children's friends want to hang out at. That means having a lot of food on hand as well as having lots of things for all of the kids to do.

While my girls were growing up, I wanted to make sure that their friends knew they were always welcome at my home, that they were loved, and that they could count on my family to help them.

Inviting Friends To Tag Along

When you plan time with your children, don't make it exclusive. Invite their friends to come along as well. While you may think that the kids will want to go off by themselves, this is actually a surefire way that they will spend time with you, especially when they're older.

One summer I took Whitney and her best friend on a senior trip to Los Angeles. We called it the "Whitney and Charity Shopping Extravaganza." We shopped until we dropped and had a blast. I not only spent money on Whitney but also on Charity. I regularly invest in the lives of my daughters' friends. I know that I can't out give God.

There are things my daughters are believing God for, and I help them out as much as I can. But

Everybody's Welcome

I purposely sow into the lives of young people so others will be there to help my daughters when they need it.

One of the best ways to win your kids over is to be kind to their friends. Doing this opens the door for them to include you in their lives. My daughters and their friends still invite me to do things with them. We go to the movies, to Starbucks, and even try out new restaurants together. This happens because I took the time to welcome their friends into my home.

Chapter 12

Respecting Authority

The Apostle Paul admonishes us to pray for those who are in authority. (1 Tim. 2:1,2.) Why? So we might lead a quiet and peaceable life. Many people fail to realize that it's God who sets people in places of authority. While you may not *like* the person who holds an office, you at least need to respect him because of the office he holds.

Number 11: Don't open the door for rebellion in your children's lives by rebelling against authority yourself.

Children are great at telling part of the story and keeping important information to themselves. You, therefore, shouldn't necessarily believe what they tell you happened in church or at school before getting all of the facts. Just because you've heard one side of the story, doesn't mean that you should call the school and be ugly to the staff.

Playing Detective

Over the years, I've developed some of the greatest investigative techniques from being a children's pastor as well as being a dad. My advice to parents is to always listen to both sides of the story before making a decision.

I wish I had a nickel for every time a parent said to me, "I know my child. He or she wouldn't do that." Even though they live in the same house, many parents don't know their children, and they're not doing them a favor by always taking their side. Siding with the Word of God and with authority is always the right thing to do.

There is always more than one side to every story. And in church, there can be hundreds of sides. Before you fly off the handle because of what you're told, do some research. Many times the fault doesn't lie on the side of authority. If your kids see that you never side with authority, you are actually opening the door for rebellion to develop in their lives.

I know a lot of adults who have bad attitudes toward authority figures, especially the police. Now I don't like to get tickets; but if I would only slow down, I wouldn't get one. If you constantly talk bad about the police, your children will follow your lead and develop a rebellious attitude toward authority. Respecting authority goes beyond the police. It also includes teachers, bosses, and all levels of governmental offices. I respect my president. Even when we had a president in office who was unfaithful and was not truthful, I still respected the office he held.

Because I want to teach my children to side with authority, I will do anything to serve my country and my president, regardless of whether or not I voted for him. By setting the example of siding with authority, my kids were taught the proper respect for all positions of authority.

Chapter 13

Take a Chill Pill

The strictest parents are usually the ones who were hellions while growing up, and they want to make sure that their kids don't follow their footsteps. In raising children, it's important to remember that there are a lot of give-and-takes. After you have set boundaries for your children, give them some breathing room. If you try to constantly monitor their every movement, you'll only cause them to leave home as soon as they can. Kids who have come out of strict environments often do everything their parents forbade them to do while growing up.

Number 12: Don't exasperate your children.

In the fifth and sixth chapters of Ephesians, Paul gives instructions to husbands, wives, and children on how they should treat one another. In Ephesians 6:4, he directs fathers to not exasperate their children but to instead "...bring them up in the training and instruction of the Lord."

The word *exasperate* means "to excite the anger of, to cause irritation or annoyance to."[5] There are many fathers who annoy their kids and cause them irritation. One way to not do this is to never forget what it was like to be a teenager.

A Watchful Eye

All children need to have set boundaries. If you tell them to be home at 10 o'clock, they shouldn't think that they can come strolling in past midnight. Likewise, if they tell you they're going to the football game, you shouldn't bump into them at the mall. After the household rules have been set, give your children opportunities to earn your trust. That means that you're not constantly breathing down their necks but that you do check up on them.

Take a Chill Pill

As teenagers, when my girls went out with their friends, I often checked to see if they were where they told me they would be. I've left notes on the car, and I've gone to the restaurant where they were eating. When they saw me, they'd ask what I was doing there. I'd say, "Just checking to make sure you were here." When your kids know that you periodically check up on them, they're more likely to always be where they tell you they are going.

A Fitting Punishment

If you do find out that your kids aren't doing what they said they would be doing, let the punishment fit the crime. If you ground them for six months for not cleaning their room, what punishment will you give them for doing something major, like grand theft auto?

Many parents, more often than not, need to take a chill pill. I had to learn that the hard way. One time I complained to my wife, "Yancy is acting just like a ten-year-old." Julie looked at me in

exasperation and said, "She is a ten-year-old."
"Oh," I said, "no wonder."

Remember, kids are kids, and part of being a kid is having a nonchalant and carefree attitude. Children live in the present and usually don't think more than five minutes into the future. Learn to be patient, and try not to be too hard on them as they learn how to be responsible and obedient.

Conclusion

You may be thinking, *I've blown some or all of these points. Now what?* We've all made mistakes, but it's never too late to begin making right choices concerning your family. I don't care what ages your kids are; it's never too late to start doing the right thing.

The first step in making changes is to identify the areas that you need to improve in. Then put actions to your decision to get things right. If you need to go to your children and apologize, do that. Or maybe you just need to really listen to them when they talk to you. Pick the ball up wherever you dropped it.

I believe your kids are worth it. I want all children to be reached with the gospel, but especially the ones who live at my house. If that's your desire too, never forget that you are the key ingredient to making it happen.

Endnotes

[1] *Merriam-Webster OnLine Dictionary,* copyright © 2002, s.v. "way"; available from <http://www.m-w.com>.

[2] *Webster's OnLine,* s.v. "manner."

[3] *Webster's OnLine,* s.v. "encourage."

[4] *Webster's OnLine,* s.v. "repent."

[5] *Webster's OnLine,* s.v. "exasperate."

Prayer of Salvation

God loves you—no matter who you are or what your past is. He loves you so much that He gave His one and only begotten Son for you. The Bible tells us "...whoever believes in him shall not perish but have eternal life" (John 3:16). Jesus laid down His life and rose again so that we could spend eternity with Him in heaven and experience His absolute best on earth. If you would like to receive Jesus into your life, say the following prayer out loud and mean it from your heart.

Heavenly Father, I come to You admitting that I am a sinner. Right now, I choose to turn away from sin, and I ask You to cleanse me of all unrighteousness. I believe that Your Son, Jesus, died on the cross to take away my sins. I also believe that He rose again from the dead so that I might be forgiven of my sins and be made righteous through faith in Him. I call upon the name of Jesus Christ to be the Savior and Lord of my life. Jesus, I choose to follow You and ask that You fill me with the power of the Holy Spirit. I declare that I am a child of God. I am free from sin and full of the righteousness of God. I am saved in Jesus' name. Amen.

If you prayed this prayer to receive Jesus Christ as your Savior, please contact us at our Web site at www.harrisonhouse.com to receive a free book.

Or you may write to us at
Harrison House
P.O. Box 35035
Tulsa, Oklahoma 74153

Meet Jim Wideman

The Past: Jim came to the Lord at the age of 17 during the Jesus movement. While in pursuit of a professional music career, he answered God's call to reach young people. For the past 25 years, he has served as a children's pastor in four different churches. He is the creator and innovator of many products and resources for children's ministry, including "Puppet Trax." In January 1986, the International Network of Children's Pastors awarded Jim the "Excellence in Children's Ministry Award." In March of 2001, *Children's Ministry Magazine* named Jim as one of the ten pioneers of the decade in children's ministry.

The Present: Jim serves under his pastor and mentor Willie George, senior pastor of the 12,000-member Church On The Move in Tulsa, Oklahoma. Jim oversees one of America's largest local children's ministries, reaching more than 3,500 children each week. He also heads up Willie George Ministries' worldwide outreaches, which include all children's ministry training events and the International Curriculum Exchange or Ice Box, a ministry that provides resources and training to children's workers in third world countries. He is the author and columnist for *Group Publishing* and *Children's Ministry Magazine.* He is host of "The Club," a children's ministers' leadership audio resource series that is listened to by hundreds of children's and youth leaders each month.

His Passion: Jim's passion can be summed up in three simple words: building strong leaders. His life's quest is "to raise up a generation of leaders who love Jesus and their pastors and who will accomplish their God-given purpose for being placed on this earth."

Personal: Jim is still deeply in love with Julie, his wife and partner of 25 years. Along with his wife, he has raised two daughters who love God, Yancy, 23, and Whitney, 19. He is an avid guitar player with an amazing collection of Fender, Gibson, and Taylor guitars and basses.

To contact Jim Wideman
please write to:

Jim Wideman
P.O. Box 1214
Broken Arrow, OK 74013

Or visit him on the Web at:
www.jimwideman.com

*Please include your prayer requests
and comments when you write.*

www.harrisonhouse.com

Fast. Easy. Convenient!

- ◆ New Book Information
- ◆ Look Inside the Book
- ◆ Press Releases
- ◆ Bestsellers

- ◆ Free E-News
- ◆ Author Biographies
- ◆ Upcoming Books
- ◆ Share Your Testimony

For the latest in book news and author information, please visit us on the Web at www.harrisonhouse.com. Get up-to-date pictures and details on all our powerful and life-changing products. Sign up for our e-mail newsletter, *Friends of the House,* and receive free monthly information on our authors and products including testimonials, author announcements, and more!

Harrison House—
Books That Bring Hope, Books That Bring Change

The Harrison House Vision

Proclaiming the truth and the power

Of the Gospel of Jesus Christ

With excellence;

Challenging Christians to

Live victoriously,

Grow spiritually,

Know God intimately.